C000117058

the little book of

MINDFULNESS II

Hardie Grant

QUADRILLE

"Always hold fast to the present. Every situation, indeed every moment, is of infinite value, for it is the representative of a whole eternity."

JOHANN WOLFGANG VON GOETHE

Definition of Mindfulness

1. The quality or state of being mindful.

2. The practice of maintaining a non-judgemental state of heightened or complete awareness of one's thoughts, emotions or experiences on a moment-to-moment basis; also such a state of awareness.

Mindfulness: a soothing concoction of attention, awareness, curiosity and openness, blended with love and a lightness of spirit, and served with a smile.

"Remember that there is only one important time and it is Now. The present moment is the only time over which we have dominion."

LEO TOLSTOY
From *The Three Questions*

Mindfulness challenges us to wake up, to see and appreciate the joy, to experience each second vividly, rather than sleepwalking through existence. Be the captain of the ship and take the helm; master yourself and you will master mindfulness.

"The strength of a man's virtue should not be measured by his special exertions, but by his habitual acts."

BLAISE PASCAL

"Mindfulness is the doorway to live in harmony with the Universe."

AMIT RAY

Manifest Harmony

Consider where your focus lies. It's easy to get caught up in the things that don't matter, to wander from the path of peace. Arguments can escalate at the drop of a hat and become much bigger if we put our time and energy into them. Switch your focus and know that all things pass. Moods change, emotions ebb and fall, night follows day and the wheel keeps turning.

"Suffering is not holding you. You are holding suffering. When you become good at the art of letting sufferings go, then you'll come to realize how unnecessary it was for you to drag those burdens around with you. You'll see that no one else other than you was responsible. The truth is that existence wants your life to become a festival."

OSHO

The Two Wolves

There are two wolves inside us. One is evil, made up of hate, anger, despair and jealousy. The other is good, a creature of joy, peace, kindness and love. Together they battle for supremacy, and while it is a constant struggle for all mankind, the wolf that wins is always the one you feed.

Parable attributed to Native American tribe – either Cherokee or Lenape, no one knows for sure.

"It is not our purpose to become each other; it is to recognize each other, to learn to see the other and honour him for what he is."

HERMANN HESSE
From *Narziß und Goldmund*
(*Narcissus and Goldmund*)

Take a Step Back

If you find yourself in the middle of an argument, don't get caught up in hateful words. Take a deep breath and shout 'Stop!' in your head. As you look at the person, imagine your gaze falling back inside your head.

If it helps, take a physical step back. See the person for what they are: a human being in need of love and someone who is struggling at this moment to express themselves.

Bring your attention to the back of your head with every breath, until you feel calm and able to see the situation for what it is – a moment in passing.

"The good life is a process, not a state of being. It is a direction not a destination."

CARL ROGERS
From *On Becoming a Person*

"The world is big and I want to have a good look at it before it gets dark."

JOHN MUIR

Life is like a giant Ferris wheel. Go up and the view is awesome. Come down and there's not much to see, but just as you're feeling a sense of despair, the wheel moves again. Ever so slightly it turns, until once more you feel a rush of excitement – liberation is at hand. You're on the up, and the dark moment that once held you so tightly in its grip is behind you.

The Mindful Home

Colours are a delight to the eye and have a soothing effect on the mind. Evidence suggests that the hues we surround ourselves with have an influence on mood and emotional health. Certain shades stimulate a positive response in the brain, while others can trigger agitation. Create a mindful home by opting for shades that make you feel calm, balanced and joyful.

"There is no sanctuary of virtue like home."

EDWARD EVERETT

Design is a form of escapism; create a safe space to decompress, disconnect and evaluate.

Curiosity cannot be penned in. It lives in the imagination and at the forefront of dreams, flowing out of us with a look, a voice, a touch. This wonder is the key to learning about ourselves and the world around us, and with this enlightenment, comes peace.

" The important thing is to not stop questioning. Curiosity has its own reason for existing."

ALBERT EINSTEIN

"Curiosity is the lust of the mind."

THOMAS HOBBES

"Curiosity is the wick in the candle of learning."

WILLIAM ARTHUR WARD

Balancing all of life's demands can be stressful and time-consuming.

The Swedish word *lagom* means not too little, not too much. Just right.

With this in mind, find your balance, keeping in mind that this often involves removing the negative and embracing the simple, most important things in life.

Finding Balance

Begin with the home and the rest of life will follow.

You don't need a multitude of 'things'. Curate your home to be a functional, beautiful and calm space.

Things to ask yourself:
Do I need this?
Does this make me happy?
Could I live without this?

Home, like a mother's womb, should be a retreat, a haven and a place of power.

"A home... is a kingdom of its own in the midst of the world; a stronghold amid life's storms and stresses; a refuge, even a sanctuary."

DIETRICH BONHOEFFER

Bedroom

Align your body clock to the natural world and wake with the sun. Throw back the curtains and embrace the sustaining energy of those early-morning rays

Keep the room light and airy, so that it becomes a mindful sanctuary.

Make your bed every day. It is a reflection of where you're at in your head, so keep it clean, neatly turned out and ready for when sleep calls. Do this first thing, to get you in a positive and organised frame of mind for the day ahead.

Kitchen

Empty sink, empty mind. Do the dishes with diligence, putting all your attention into scrubbing and rinsing. As you do this imagine you're cleaning away any negative thoughts or stresses.

A dripping tap is a distraction and a drain to the finances. Silence the drip in your sink and in your mind. Turn negative thought patterns off, just as you would the taps in your kitchen.

Living Room

Manage the flow of energy. Take a step back and assess your living room. Does it look cluttered? Are there areas where you're tight on space? Address these issues by tidying and clearing. Remove over-large furniture and replace with something that sits easily in the space you have.

Bring the outside in by choosing natural materials that help you connect with nature. Cut flowers or a lustrous plant make a difference and change the vibe of a room.

Bathroom

Wash away the day with a clean, fresh and calm bathroom. The bathroom is a space for private meditation in what is often a busy world. Take the time to look after yourself and a positive attitude will follow.

Scented candles, bath oils and soft, fluffy towels are small changes that make a big difference to your overall sense of calm. Draw yourself a hot bath and let the steam envelope you. Any stresses will melt away and disappear down the plug hole.

The path to a more mindful life doesn't have to be a solitary one. Our lives are intertwined with a whole support network of people so embrace everything they have to offer.

Studies show that those who go through a stressful experience in the company of friends and family have lower levels of the stress hormone cortisol than those who go through such things alone.

When life gets tough, take your foot off the gas. Stop and bring to mind your nearest and dearest. Feel the love that links you and let it envelope you in a protective circle. Know that, whatever happens, you are always loved.

"*Be like the bird who, pausing in her flight awhile on boughs too slight, feels them give way beneath her, and yet sings, knowing she hath wings.*"

VICTOR HUGO
Be Like the Bird

Mindfulness helps you find value
in the small and the mundane.
Embrace the little things.

Awake with the Sun

There is no purer light than that of the morning sun when you first open your eyes. Resisting this urge to wake when the day breaks can add stress and leave you feeling out of sync. Try to rise with the sun and notice the difference in your productivity and balance.

"Believe me, all of you, the best way to help the places we live in is to be glad we live there."

EDITH WHARTON

"Live the actual moment.
Only this moment is life."

THICH NHÂT HẠNH

" The chief pleasure in eating does not consist in costly seasoning, or exquisite flavour, but in yourself."

HORACE

Thankful Toast

At every meal give thanks, out loud or in your head. Consider the food before you, and the love and energy that went into growing and preparing the dish. Consider how it will taste before your first mouthful, how nourishing it will be and what a delight it is to be sustained in this way. Postpone the physical pleasure of eating for a moment longer and revel in the anticipation of what is to come. Savour the intention to eat and make every meal an occasion for celebration.

Savour every mouthful.

Chew slowly.

Pause between each bite.

Smell every element.

Taste every flavour.

Enjoy.

Pay full attention to the experience of eating and drinking – to the colours, smells, textures, flavours and even the sounds of your food.

Notice how eating affects our mood and consider how our emotions change when we eat.

Try eating one meal a week mindfully, alone and in silence.

Let food be a rainbow on your plate and a carnival in your mouth.

Eating an array of different coloured fruit and vegetables is of huge health benefit.

Each specific hue has a variety of vitamins, minerals, antioxidants and phytochemicals that offer a range of healing properties.

Become aware of your body after you have eaten.

We often feel unsatisfied unless we are feeling full. Give your body time to rest and digest before plying it with more food.

Through being conscious of our bodies and eating habits we can interrupt our habitual overeating.

"Eating and reading are two pleasures that combine admirably."

C.S. LEWIS
From *Surprised by Joy*

Savour each mouthful as if it were your last. As you relax into the taste, texture and the rhythmic flow of the chew, let the words also flow in your mind: 'sweet,' 'silky,' 'smooth,' 'spicy,' 'zingy,' etc.

Mindful Movies

Breathe new life into movie nights with a touch of mindfulness. Choose a film you've enjoyed before and give it a rerun. Consider how you feel at various points in the movie. Notice the different emotions that play out and which characters you identify with. At the end, ask yourself what you enjoyed the most and what the film means to you. Connecting with the flow of your emotions in this way adds colour and depth to the experience.

" The moment one gives close attention to anything, even a blade of grass, it becomes a mysterious, awesome, indescribably magnificent world in itself."

HENRY MILLER

"A film is – or should be – more like music than like fiction. It should be a progression of moods and feelings. The theme, what's behind the emotion, the meaning, all that comes later."

STANLEY KUBRICK

"And into the forest I go, to lose my mind and find my soul."

JOHN MUIR

In Japan the practice of *shinrin-yoku* – 'taking in the forest atmosphere' or 'forest bathing' – first appeared in the 1980s.

The forest bather slowly walks or sits beneath the trees with no aim other than to be in tune with their senses and breathe in the forest air. This practice has a calming and rejuvenating effect enabling the bather to enjoy the time spent with nature, among the trees.

Take a walk and hold your head high. Imagine breathing in your surroundings. What can you see, smell, hear, taste and touch? How does this make you feel inside? What words would you use to describe the experience? What about music? Is there an orchestra playing in your head? Feel the beat and the rhythm of the environment beneath your feet and how it moves you.

"Flowers are restful to look at. They have neither emotions nor conflicts."

SIGMUND FREUD

Flower Power

Blossoming flowers trigger happy brain chemicals like dopamine, oxytocin and serotonin. The ancients saw fresh blooms as a sign of an abundant crop, but today it still signals the arrival of something special and creates a sense of pride in the eye of the beholder.

" To see a World in a Grain of Sand
And a Heaven in a Wild Flower,
Hold Infinity in the palm of your hand
And Eternity in an hour."

WILLIAM BLAKE
From *Auguries of Innocence*

"God Almighty first planted a garden. And indeed it is the purest of human pleasures."

FRANCIS BACON
From *Of Gardens: An Essay*

Consider your garden an artist's canvas, a place where you can work in harmony with nature and express who you are. Every moment spent in the sanctuary of outdoor space is an opportunity to get to know yourself, to live not only in the moment but in sync with the earth.

Take a moment to notice the little things. The hum of a bee; the crunch of leaves under foot; the dew glistening on a spider's web.

Even the smallest things play a part in the world around us.

Cynefin is a welsh word meaning a place where a person or animal feels it ought to live and belong; it is where the natural world around you feels right and welcoming.

Smell the Roses

What could be better than engaging your senses in the garden.

Stand and feel the warm breeze of spring.

Close your eyes and inhale the gentle fragrance of a flower in summer. How does it make you feel?

Kick a pile of autumn leaves, engaging your inner child.

Wrap up warm and brace yourself against the frosty air of winter.

"Look deep into nature and you will understand everything better."

ALBERT EINSTEIN

Mindful Gardening

Dig with purpose. Feel the strength of your muscles as the tip of the spade hits the soil. Recognise your intention to mould the earth into a space where you can plant with ease.

Dip your hands into the soil. Feel it crumbling between your fingers. Notice how moist it is, rich with nutrients and ready to support the seeds and bulbs you sow.

Bathe each plant in glistening drops of water. Notice how this changes the colour of the leaves and petals, giving them a vibrant glow. Imagine the water sinking deep into the earth to nourish the roots as you do this.

Keep track of the seasons. Notice the subtle changes as the weather turns and different plants and wildlife appear. Appreciate a frosty morning just as much as you would the warmth of the sun.

Experience new life. Marvel at seeds that bring shoots into being. Tend to your seedlings and feel proud that your efforts have created something living.

Turn your compost. Feel the heat that radiates from it and smell its earthy richness. Full of organic life, this will provide your garden with the nutrients it needs to remain healthy.

"I have never had so many good ideas day after day as when I worked in the garden."

JOHN ERSKINE

" The least movement is of importance to all nature. The entire ocean is affected by a pebble."

BLAISE PASCAL

Plant mint in your garden and crush the leaves as you wander past. The aroma will instantly refresh you.

Many cultures use mint in recipes, from strong peppermints for teas to spearmints used in cooking.

Mint is invasive in the garden, so grow each type in its own pot and keep moist.

*"All my hurt my garden spade
can heal."*

RALPH WALDO EMERSON

Reconnect

Turn off your phone and stand outside.

Notice the earth, feel the soil, smell the air and take a long, slow, deep breath.

Connect with the world around you.

"Your mind is your garden,
your thoughts are the seeds,
the harvest can either be flowers
or weeds."

WILLIAM WORDSWORTH

"When Great Spirit created the world, all things were equal. Animals were skin-walkers, fluid beings able to shift between human and animal form. But while their human skins gave them flexibility and the gift of words, it also cursed them with an ego. This in turn created deceitful tendencies and petty jealousies. They demanded to know who the best creature was, who was worthy of the title 'King of the Animals'. This both angered and saddened Great Spirit. In answer, he took away their human form, cast it out into the world to walk as something new.

From that day forwards animals never walked on two legs or spoke in human tongue again, but neither were they plagued by the fickle weaknesses of mankind."

NATIVE AMERICAN TALE

There is a lot we can learn from the animal kingdom. Simply observing different animals and how they behave is enough to put you in a mindful state.

Remember that everything you do doesn't affect just the human population, but the animal one too.

Be mindful of the effect our actions have on animals and our connection to the natural world.

*"Some people talk to animals.
Not many listen, though.
That's the problem."*

A.A. MILNE

"Animals are such agreeable friends – they ask no questions, they pass no criticisms."

GEORGE ELIOT
From *Mr Gilfil's Love Story*

Animals have a much simpler way of life, without the complexities of modern humans. Take inspiration from them and get in touch with your primal side.

Observe and Immerse

Go for a walk, somewhere like your local park or a favourite spot in the countryside. As you stroll, make a point of being aware not just of your surroundings, but of other signs of life. Listen for the rustle of leaves, the sounds of birdsong, the gentle flap of wings or a bee buzzing as it settles on a flower. Look for movement too: the scamper of a squirrel as it scales a branch, the twitching of tiny beetle legs as they navigate the forest floor.

Observe how each creature moves and makes the most of the landscape. Sit and watch. Take everything in with each breath. Let thoughts come and go as you appreciate the sheer beauty of the natural world.

Mindful Creatures

Take things a step further and focus on one creature. Notice how perfectly it is made to suit its environment. Consider its natural rhythm and how it engages with the surroundings. Then consider how you are constructed, and how amazing the human body is. Bring to mind the abilities you have and how you can engage more with your surroundings and make the most of your gifts and talents.

Look to the animal kingdom for a masterclass in mindfulness. Every creature lives in the moment, fully aware of how they feel and what is going on around them. Survival is key, which means each second counts, and holds the potential for great adventure. Our pets can teach us much, whether you're a feline fan or a dog devotee, (perhaps guinea pigs make your heart sing) – it doesn't matter the size or type of animal – there's a lesson there.

"Until one has loved an animal, a part of one's soul remains unawakened."

ANATOLE FRANCE

Studies show that cuddling or stroking a pet releases the 'cuddle hormone' oxytocin in both human and pet. This has a soothing effect on the mind and body which is conducive to meditation and mindfulness practice.

Mindful Moments

If you're blessed with a furry friend
who enjoys a cuddle, use this time
for some mindfulness practice. It will
strengthen the bond you have and
help you appreciate each other while
calming mind, body and soul.

"People need to know that they have all the tools within themselves. Self-awareness, which means awareness of their body, awareness of their mental space, awareness of their relationships – not only with each other, but with life and the ecosystem."

DEEPAK CHOPRA

What qualities in animals do you admire? Try to mimic them.

It is because of the good of his heart
that the crab has no head.

CREOLE PROVERB

Conscious Commuting

Turn the time you travel to and from work from a curse into a blessing with a mindful approach to your commute.

"I love commuting between languages just like I love commuting between cultures and cities."

ELIF ŞAFAK

Bus, Tube or Train

Sit back in your chair. Press the base of your spine into the seat, then imagine a thread running up your spine and out of the top of your head. Feel this thread gently pulling so that your spine lengthens. Roll your shoulders back and breathe. Let your mind wander as your gaze settles on fellow travellers and the passing scenery. Remember, everyone has their own story, so instead of ignoring those who share your journey, be mindful of them. Offer a smile. Be aware of their needs.

Car

See other car drivers as companions on the road and don't let niggles get out of hand. Like worker bees, each driver is on a mission to reach his or her destination, and like anyone set on a target, can easily forget that others have their own path. Be aware of how you feel in every moment, so that you recognise anger before it flares. Then make a choice and ask yourself: do I want to feel stressed and in a bad mood, or do I want to feel relaxed?

On Foot

Even if you're hotfooting it through busy city streets you can find your zen by connecting with the rhythm of each footfall. Count it out in your mind as you walk. Focus on the feeling of the ground beneath your feet and how you connect with it. Anchor yourself with every step and notice how the earth supports you. Take in the air and feel yourself float through it.

There is power in words. Place them together with thought and passion to form a fresh perspective.

"Attitude is a little thing that makes a big difference."

WINSTON CHURCHILL

Commute with confidence

Give yourself an affirmation each morning. This could be something you choose each day to help you meet your goals, like 'Today success is mine' or a general mantra for wellbeing like 'I love my life and it loves me.' Pinpoint visual cues along your journey that are important to you. For example, you might pass a beautiful old church that always catches your eye, or a particular tree that stands out from the others.

Work it out

Your work life can be stressful and tiring. It's important to learn how to balance the professional and personal. Dreams and goals take hard work and perseverance but it's also important to maintain a mindful approach and take time out for yourself.

Choose a job you love and you will never have to work a day in your life.

Work-life Balance

Designate time periods for email
checking – for example, first thing
in the morning, midday and late
afternoon. Make this a part of your
routine until it becomes habit.

Retract, don't React.

It's easy to misconstrue the sentiment or meaning of an email, so rather than firing out a snappy retort, take a minute and breathe. Take some time away from the screen and let emotions settle.

If you feel the urge to respond in haste, type something out, then send it to yourself; this allows you to be objective. Reread and notice how the email makes you feel.

Positive Affirmations

Compose an email of positive affirmations and encouraging quotes. Send it to yourself, then take a minute every day to read it.

- Today will be productive and fulfilling.

- Be patient and persistent.

- I will make this day count.

- Each day I am learning and evolving.

- I will surround myself with positive energy.

- I value the balance in my life.

- My time is valuable.

- I will not take my work home with me.

- I encourage other people's success.

- I choose to respond with positivity in moments of stress.

Mindful Colleagues

Be mindful of your work colleagues. Ask them how they're really feeling. Actively listen to their response, and even if you can't think of anything to say in return, acknowledge how they're feeling. In taking time out for others, you're taking time for yourself, forging connections that will flourish in the future.

"When we listen deeply to another person, we not only recognize their wrong perceptions, but we also identify our own wrong perceptions about ourselves and about the other person. That is why mindful dialogue and mindful communication are crucial to removing anger and violence."

THICH NHAT HANH

Mindful Communications

If there is an important meeting or conversation you need to have which may be tricky, try these three mindful techniques to help you feel relaxed, focused and able to express yourself.

Visualise

Before arriving at your meeting or engagement, visualise how you'd like it to go. Run through the conversation in your head, making it the best-case scenario. See yourself fully engaging with the people present, actively listening to what they have to say. Note how the conversation flows with ease.

Arrive Fully

Often the body is present when the mind is not. To arrive fully in the moment and be ready to engage in communication, we first need to breathe, and make some physical changes.

Ensure that your posture is open and alert. Position your feet shoulder-width apart and spread the weight evenly between them. Allow your stomach to relax gently and lengthen so that your spine stretches and you find it easier to take deep breaths. Let your gaze soften, which in turn releases tension from your brow. Smile.

Actively Listen and Digest

To listen, you don't have to hear every word, but you do have to understand the underlying themes and motivations being expressed. To ensure your attention is focused, imagine drawing a circle around you and the person/people you're with. This will help you direct your attention to that moment. Soften your chest by imagining a lump of ice gradually melting as you breathe.

"Every time there's a new tool, whether it's internet or cell phones or anything else, all these things can be used for good or evil. Technology is neutral; it depends on how it's used."

RICK SMOLAN

Smartphone, Smart Thinking

See your smartphone as a mindful tool by using it with purpose. Set a reminder throughout the day. Every time it pings, it's a call to arms: a moment to catch yourself, check on your thoughts and feelings, and breathe with meaning.

Disconnect, switch off, look up:
the world is waiting.

*"Keep your face to the sunshine
and you cannot see a shadow."*

HELEN KELLER

Mindless = not caring much.

Mindful = caring a lot.

From Mindless to Mindful

Be more aware of when you're holding and looking at your phone. Learn to notice how it feels in your hands. How does it feel when you look at it? What muscles do you use? Pay attention to your eyes. Do they feel sore/tired? What are you really seeing? Give yourself a break by tearing your gaze away to something new and focusing on that for a minute. The more you practise this, the more aware and less automated you'll become when reaching for your phone

"Between stimulus and response there is a space. In that space is our power to choose our response. In our response lies our growth and our freedom."

VIKTOR FRANKL

Focus on Yourself

Everyone needs to take some 'me time' away from social media to recuperate and realign.

This could be as simple as taking a few minutes to sit down and read a book, take a bath or going for a walk in the fresh air.

Mindful Love

Romance is a mindful business. It's about paying attention to the space between the words, the things that remain unsaid. Act with care and purpose and appreciate the gift of the person you share your life with.

"The pursuit, even of the best things, ought to be calm and tranquil."

CICERO

"You cannot see things until you roughly know where they are."

"All the beautiful sentiments in the world weigh less than a single lovely action."

JAMES RUSSELL LOWELL

Research shows that relationships are more satisfying when mindfulness is practised. This is because individuals feel more valued, which in turn fosters intimacy, trust and a deeper connection.

Mindful Ways to Show You Care

It's easy to move through daily life and all the challenges it brings and take partnerships for granted. Write a list of all the things you love about your partner. Read it regularly to remind you of how special they are.

A humble cup of tea, made with love and presented with a smile, can be enough to show someone how much they mean to you.

Write a Love Poem

It doesn't have to be eloquent; something simple and fun means just as much, as it comes from the heart.

Listen

Instead of jumping to offer advice to problems, take a back seat and let your other half express how they feel. Allow space for them to get things off their chest and be supportive and respectful.

Be Aware

Be fully present in the things you do together. Whether you're having a nice meal at a fancy restaurant, or shopping at the supermarket, make every experience count by being aware of your partner and how they feel. Take the time to appreciate the little things.

Remember

Create a memory box and keep mementos of those special moments you've shared. Include photographs and tokens that you've gathered on your journeys together. Remember to keep adding new things to the box so that it evolves and grows like your love for each other.

"When I walk with you I feel as if I had a flower in my buttonhole."

WILLIAM MAKEPEACE THACKERAY

"True self is non-self, the awareness that the self is made only of non-self elements. There's no separation between self and other, and everything is interconnected."

THICH NHAT HANH

"Love yourself first and everything else falls into line."

LUCILLE BALL

Mindfulness and Healing

When mindfulness is in action,
the brain responds; scientists have
discovered that areas of the brain that
relate to interconnectedness light up.
This in turn activates the 'wellbeing'
region of the brain.

We are all connected. Every person we meet, every relationship we have, every part of the natural world... we are as one. Once we realise this, we can see that the vast power of the universe is ours.

"I realized that if my thoughts immediately affect my body, I should be careful about what I think. Now if I get angry, I ask myself why I feel that way. If I can find the source of my anger, I can turn that negative energy into something positive."

YOKO ONO

Prayer

A way to pay attention to our thoughts and needs. A way to nurture hopes and dreams and plant seeds of positivity.

Who do you speak to in the darkness? A spirit, an angel, a guru or guide? God, the Goddess, or the spark that dwells inside? Wherever you find comfort, know that strength and peace live in you, just a breath away, in the space between heartbeats.

Mindfulness is a way of being, not a religion. It has its origins in many ancient practices, including Buddhism, Taoism, Hinduism and Stoicism, but it does not belong to any one source. Like the breeze that slips through the window on a windy day, it touches everything, but it cannot be owned. It is free and there for everyone.

"Happiness is your nature. It is not wrong to desire it. What is wrong is seeking it outside when it is inside."

RAMANA MAHARSHI

"I think it's very healthy to spend time alone. You need to know how to be alone and not be defined by another person."

OLIVIA WILDE

"Keep knocking and the joy inside will eventually open a window and look out to see who's there."

RUMI

What makes you truly happy? Is it a place, spending time with certain people, an activity? Spend a few minutes focusing on the things that bring you joy, then bring that into the everyday by doing more of the things that make your heart sing.

Identify a place that makes you happy in your mind; this could be somewhere you've been before, or somewhere you'd like to go. It could be a tropical beach, or a spring meadow, a far-flung location, or your local park. Picture the place in your mind and imagine you are there. Engage all your senses as you do this. Feel the joy as you absorb the essence of the place. Set a reminder on your phone, so that you practise this for a few minutes every day. You'll feel brighter, lighter and bursting with vitality while able to appreciate every moment with renewed hope.

*"Perfection of character is this:
to live each day as if it were your
last, without frenzy, without apathy,
without pretence."*

MARCUS AURELIUS

Mindful Mojo

Combine the power of crystal healing with a simple meditation technique to put a spring in your step.

Quartz crystal naturally amplifies energy, making it the ideal meditation stone. Find a piece you like and hold it in both hands.

Sit on the floor and feel your body connecting to the ground beneath. Know that you are supported and energised by the earth.

Close your eyes and focus on your breath.

As you breathe in, imagine you're taking in light and love. Feel it flowing from the crystal, into your palms, along each arm and flooding your entire body with energy.

As you breathe out, imagine you're expelling negative energy. Feel it flowing from your body, through your hands into the stone.

Continue to focus on this circuit of energy and let thoughts come and go as you do this.

"Meditation can help us embrace our worries, our fear, our anger; and that is very healing. We let our own natural capacity of healing do the work."

THICH NHAT HANH

When we meditate, the integrative centre for emotional behaviour and motivation known as the amygdala region is "reset" so that it can better handle emotional processing and anger control. The change that occurs is maintained during non-meditative states.

"The ability to be in the present moment is a major component of mental wellness."

ABRAHAM MASLOW

"Don't seek, don't search, don't ask, don't knock, don't demand – relax."

OSHO

"A journey of a thousand miles begins with a single step."

LAO TZU

"Adventure is worthwhile."

ARISTOTLE

Mantras are prescriptions for the soul; affirmations that can be chanted in meditation or at any time to bring you back to the present moment.

Mindful Mantras

I give from a place of plenty.

Gratitude is my attitude.

Kindness is my currency.

Switch off to switch on.

Breathe in light and love, breathe out stress and tension.

My thoughts shape my reality.

Joy is within.

Be still, be present.

Nature nurtures my every step.

Each moment is an opportunity for me to shine my light.

Mindful Mantras

Practising mindfulness during exercise not only enhances the experience, bringing more enjoyment, it makes it more effective. By paying attention to every move, you'll ensure you do it properly and to the best of your abilities. You're less likely to injure yourself and you'll be more aware of the results.

Listen to your body's needs.

Be aware of each muscle working
in unison.

Focus on the rise and fall of your chest,
and the fluidity of each breath.

As you extend each limb, feel the
tension, the delicate pull as the
tendons tighten.

Breathe into this moment, into
the stretch.

Then enjoy the release, the feeling
of freedom that comes as the muscles
start to relax.

Try this:

Go for a run, or jog on the spot.

Breathe into each footfall.

Feel your heart beating in your chest.

Increase your strides.

Increase the speed.

Focus on your breath and notice any changes.

Steady the rhythm of your breath.

Lengthen your strides.

Notice any tension in your muscles.

Gradually slow down.

Breathe into a walk.

Pour your breath into each leg.

Come to a gentle stop.

"True enjoyment comes from activity of the mind and exercise of the body; the two are ever united."

WILHELM VON HUMBOLDT

Mindful Moderation

Moderation does not mean deprivation; it's about recognising when you have enough, whether that's food or material things. By maintaining awareness through mindfulness, we know when we've reached this point. We can identify it and respond with positive action, thus creating a healthy sense of balance.

"When you realize there is nothing lacking, the whole world belongs to you."

LAO TZU

Imagine, Engage, Create

According to legend, Michelangelo spent many days simply gazing at the rock that would become his David. With a glass of wine in one hand and a chunk of bread in the other, to all the world it looked like he had lost his creative mojo. One day, his patrons decided to question him on this lack of activity. 'We hear you've stopped working,' they said. Michelangelo replied with a smile, 'I have been working every day.'

A mindful mind is a creative mind. The space between thought and deed is a well of creativity, a vast chasm where imagination weaves its magic and inspiration brings forth new ideas and associations.

Find your passion and feed it. Treat it with care. Be mindful of your skills and practise them with purpose. Whether crafting, sewing, baking, painting or writing, whatever it is, be in the moment with it. For in giving it your full attention, you slip mysteriously and delightfully into the creative zone, where all things are possible.

Everything you do, do from the heart.

The Dutch word *prutsen* means to do something which to others may have little significance, but to you, it means the world.

" Everything you can imagine is real."

PABLO PICASSO

Mindful Daydreaming

Research has discovered that 'positive constructive daydreaming' is associated with playful thoughts that encompass wish fulfilment, without psychological conflict. This type of daydreaming is not about distracting oneself from a task; neither is it tainted with anxiety or negative thoughts. So while daydreaming is often seen as the enemy of mindfulness, it is, if enjoyed in a mindful way, hugely rewarding and beneficial.

"*A daydream is a meal at which images are eaten. Some of us are gourmets, some gourmands, and a good many take their images precooked out of a can and swallow them down whole, absent-mindedly and with little relish.*"

W.H. AUDEN

Make daydreaming a purposeful act, so that, while your mind might be wandering, you are in control of its exploits and can direct it to positive, uplifting musings.

Your past is not your future.

Mindful Slumbers

According to a 2015 study published in the journal JAMA Internal Medicine, meditation and other mindfulness techniques are the key to a good night's sleep. The study took 49 adults with insomnia and split them into two test groups. The first group took part in a six-week mindfulness and meditation course, while the second group attended sleep-education classes also for a period of six weeks. Results clearly showed that the first group experienced less insomnia, exhaustion and depression than the second group.

"It is in our idleness, in our dreams, that the submerged truth sometimes comes to the top."

VIRGINIA WOOLF

Take a mindful approach to bedtime with these four pre-sleep checks.

1. Ensure the room is cool and well aired.

2. Ensure the room is dark; too much light can disrupt sleep patterns.

3. Switch off and remove all devices, from smartphones and laptops to TVs and any other form of technology.

4. Burn lavender-scented oil or spritz some on your pillow to encourage a relaxing slumber.

*" There is a time for many words,
and there is also a time for sleep."*

HOMER

Sleep Meditation

Think of a word you associate with sleep, like 'peace,' or 'calm'.

Repeat the word a few times out loud, then in your head.

Continue to repeat, but lower the volume and speed.

As you breathe in, imagine you're taking in peaceful energy.

As you breathe out, say the word in your head.

Extend your breathing, making both the inward and outward breath longer.

Focus on the word as you say it, and what it means to you.

Continue this cycle of breathing and focusing on the word until you drift into slumber.

*"Past and future are in the mind only –
I am now."*

SRI NISARGADATTA MAHARAJ

Be in the moment, not of it. Claim it, use it, embrace it with every part of your being.

"Begin doing what you want to do now. We are not living in eternity. We have only this moment, sparkling like a star in our hand – and melting like a snowflake."

MARIE BEYNON RAY

Wake up! Seize the day.
Realise your potential.

You are a tiny speck of light upon this earth, a dancing firefly. Make the most of every moment, for every moment is a gift. It cannot be relived or held onto. It is the here and now. Give it the attention it deserves, and happiness will be your reward.

"Be happy in the moment, that's enough. Each moment is all we need, not more."

MOTHER TERESA

"Happiness is something to do, something to love, something to hope for."

RUSSIAN PROVERB

It is what it is.

It was what it was.

It will be what it will be.

Don't stress.

"Day by day, what you choose, what you think and what you do is who you become."

HERACLITUS

Life is the biggest journey of all.

"*Whenever I feel blue,
I start breathing again.*"

L. FRANK BAUM

Breathe in. Breathe out.

BIBLIOGRAPHY & FURTHER READING

Bacon, Francis., *Of Gardens: An Essay* (1625)

Blake, William., *Auguries of Innocence* (1863)

Eliot, George., *Mr Gilfils's Love Story* (1857)

Hesse, Hermann., *Narziß und Goldmund* (Fischer Verlag, 1930)

Hugo, Victor., *Be like the Bird*

Lewis, C. S., *Out of the Silent Planet* (John Lane, 1938)

Lewis, C. S., *Surprised by Joy* (Geoffrey Bles, 1955)

Oliver, Mary., *Red Bird* (Beacon press, 2008)

Rogers, Carl., *On Becoming a Person* (1930)

Tolstoy, Leo., *The Three Questions* (1885)

QUOTES ARE TAKEN FROM:

A. A. Milne was an English author and poet best known for his work *Winnie The Pooh*.

Abraham Maslow was an American psychologist.

Albert Einstein was a theoretical physicist who developed the theory of relativity.

Amit Ray is an Indian author.

Anatole France was a French novelist, journalist and poet.

Aristotle was an ancient Greek scientist and philosopher.

Blaise Pascal was a 17th century French mathematician.

C. S. Lewis was a British author famous for his work *The Chronicles of Narnia*.

Carl Rogers was an American psychologist.

Cicero was a Roman statesman and orator.

Deepak Chopra is an American-Indian author, orator and a leader of the New Age movement.

Dietrich Bonhoeffer was a German theologian and anti-Nazi protester.

Edith Wharton was an American designer and short story writer.

Edward Everett was an American politician and orator.

Elif Şafak is a Turkish-British academic, author and women's rights activist.

Francis Bacon was an English philosopher, scientist and author.

George Eliot (pen name of Mary Anne Evans) was an English author and poet during the Victorian era.

Helen Keller was an American author and political activist and was the first deaf-blind person to earn a bachelor of arts degree.

Henry Miller was an American writer who lived in Paris.

Heraclitus was a Greek philosopher.

Hermann Hesse was a German-Swiss artist, famous for his painting, poetry and novels.

Homer was an ancient Greek writer and author of the epic poems, the *Iliad* and the *Odyssey*.

Horace was an ancient Roman poet.

James Russell Lowell was an American poet and diplomat.

Johann Wolfgang von Goethe was a German statesman and writer.

John Erskine was an American composer, pianist and author.

John Muir was a Scottish-American naturalist, environmentalist and author commonly known as 'Father of the National Parks'.

L. Frank Baum was an American author most famously known for his work *The Wizard of Oz*.

Lao Tzu was a Chinese philosopher and writer and founder of Taoism.

Leo Tolstoy was a Russian writer. His works include *War and Peace* and *Anna Karenina*.

Lucille Ball was an American producer, actress, comedian and model.

Marcus Aurelius was the Roman emperor between 161 and 180 AD.

Marie Beynon Ray was the author of several self-help books.

Mother Teresa was an Albanian-Indian Roman Catholic nun and missionary.

Olivia Wilde is an American producer, actress and activist.

Osho was an Indian public speaker, viewed as a controversial mystic during his lifetime.

Pablo Picasso was a Spanish painter and sculptor.

Ralph Waldo Emerson was an American poet and philosopher who led the transcendentalist movement.

Ramana Maharshi was a Hindu sage and jivanmukta (having achieved an inner freedom while living).

Rick Smolen is a former travel photographer who is now the CEO of Against All Odds Productions.

Rumi was a 13th Century Persian poet and Islamic scholar.

Sigmund Freud was the founder of psychoanalysis.

Sri Nisargadatta Maharaj was an Indian guru.

Stanley Kubrick was an American screenwriter, producer and director and is considered to be one of the most influential film makers of all time.

Thich Nhât Hạnh is a Vietnamese monk and peace activist.

Thomas Hobbes was a 17th century English philosopher.

Victor Hugo was a French novelist, dramatist and poet during the Romantic period.

Viktor Frankl was an Austrian neurologist and holocaust survivor.

Virginia Woolf was an English writer.

W. H. Auden was an English-American poet.

Wilhelm von Humboldt was a Prussian philosopher and diplomat.

William Arthur Ward was an American writer specialising in public relations.

William Blake was a British painter and poet during the Romantic Age.

William Makepeace Thackeray was a British satirical novelist, famous for his work *Vanity Fair*.

William Wordsworth was an English poet during the Romantic Age.

Winston Churchill was Prime Minister of the United Kingdom from 1940–1945 and 1951–1955.

Yoko Ono is a Japanese singer-songwriter and peace activist.

Publishing Director Sarah Lavelle
Editor Harriet Butt
Assistant Editor Harriet Webster
Words Alison Davies, Joanna Gray
Series Designer Emily Lapworth
Designer Monika Adamczyk
Production Director Vincent Smith
Production Controller Sinead Hering

Published in 2019 by Quadrille,
an imprint of Hardie Grant Publishing

Quadrille
52–54 Southwark Street
London SE1 1UN
quadrille.com

Cataloguing in Publication Data: a
catalogue record for this book is available
from the British Library.

ISBN 978 1 78713 380 8

Printed in China